T0125369

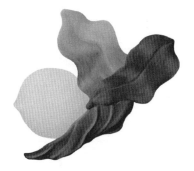

because the sun

the

sun

SARAH BURGOYNE

COACH HOUSE BOOKS, TORONTO

Canada Council **Conseil des Arts**
for the Arts **du Canada**

Published with the generous assistance of the Canada Council for the Arts
and the Ontario Arts Council. Coach House Books also acknowledges the
support of the Government of Canada through the Canada Book Fund and
the Government of Ontario through the Ontario Book Publishing Tax Credit.

LIBRARY AND ARCHIVES CANADA CATALOGUING IN PUBLICATION

Title: Because the sun / Sarah Burgoyne.
Names: Burgoyne, Sarah, author.
Description: Poems.
Identifiers: Canadiana (print) 20210156740 | Canadiana (ebook)
20210156813 | ISBN 9781552454237 (softcover) | ISBN 9781770566705
(EPUB) | ISBN 9781770566712 (PDF)
Classification: LCC PS8603.U73715 B43 2021 | DDC C811/.6—dc23

Because the Sun is available as an ebook: ISBN 978 1 77056 670 5 (EPUB);
978 1 77076 671 2 (PDF)

Purchase of the print version of this book entitles you to a free digital copy.
To claim your ebook of this title, please email sales@chbooks.com with proof
of purchase. (Coach House Books reserves the right to terminate the free
digital download offer at any time.)

Dialogue.

'And what do you do in life?'

'I count.'

'What?'

'I count. I say: one, the sea; two, the sky (ah, how beautiful it is); three, women; four, flowers (ah, how happy I am).'

ALBERT CAMUS

TABLE OF CONTENTS

THE WHOLE TIME, THE SUN.[1]

When we get out of the car, we stare at each other without blinking.

It was this burning, which I couldn't stand anymore, that made me move forward.[2]

The sun on our upturned faces dries the last of the water trickling into our mouths.[3]

All we can feel are the cymbals of sunlight crashing on our heads and, indistinctly, a dazzling spear flying up in front of us.[4]

Pain makes us pay attention; we watch our bodies.[5]

Take a closer look at the world. What hurts.

The day, already bright with sun, hit us like a slap in the face.[6]

1. Camus, Albert. *The Stranger*. Translated by Matthew Ward. New York: Random House, 1993.

2. Ibid.

3. Ibid.

4. Ibid.

5. Ahmed, Sara. *The Cultural Politics of Emotion*. New York: Routledge, 2015.

6. Camus, Albert. *The Stranger*.

one, the sun

WHAT COMES AFTER

the sun is always meaning   giving already (on)going
    (never not the sun)   *how we experience a* _____
        as familiar;   the sun   this spot
    this spot determiner   (am i hearing from you?)
    the sun offers   standards

sun sun soon

ongoing

☀

here is where i work:
        cause (a wound, injury, or person) to sound
and i work here   the plodder

through the fat park   this concern   *being*
the ball kicked to the sun (is to heal?)   *being as i am*

a woman

synonyms: make/get better, make/get well, (be) cure(d),
    treat (to) recover, restore to men(d), (im)prove, more?

who needs things

worse, harms
like every person *become sound*
or healthy again   having (had) them all
i am rich to wait until _____ *had healed*
the sun is back   (had healed)
antonyms: get worse

☀

alleviate   here it comes
(a person's distress or anguish)
carrying such old toys   *despairing of you*
'when electrocuted, time can _____ the pain of grief'
correct or put right   (hover in this).
'the rift between them was never really _____'

[marie] began to _____
saying *it wasn't like that*
there was more to it
that she was being forced
to say

le contraire

☀

(14)

synonyms: put right, set right, repair, remedy, resolve,
     correct, settle; more?
thank you
old hornet nest in a tree
what i haven't been to
(to think this)

antonyms: worsen
this side, lately   the action
of restoring
(i was sent here to write this)
i am strung under the sun

someone charts the distance
i move about   a
(normal life, impr_____)
h____   h_____
(breathh,

                    take a slow ride around me)

what comes after?
hher walking within three weeks
this is me, unable to make of thhis again

                              ✳

the action of restoring someone to former privileges
here where i remeet thee

in this moment, i am a cone
my reputation   divided into squares of sidewalk
i swirl at my base
point to a tip
a period of disfavour
no, please don't talk to me

the top
divides again with cracks

☀

'rehabilitation of the activist'
move me to the river

the action of restoring something that
i just can't keep carrying
'rehabilitation of the mangrove forests'
_____ *keeps returning*

☀

not punting but hitting back
resurge 'to rise again'   rise again

lift oneself
reclimbing the mountain to its crag (the forest drowns
out the plane that returns)
is restored
from re- 'again' (see re-)

＊

i
  clamber
          what carries out to the last –
          this (year returned to its small edge)
          in the middle of its punting
          'to rise' + a pattern
          the ride's the same   in a pane of glass   sudden
          and it's the exact same spot   as the waves
          or the seeping tide

'flooding caused by tidal surges'
the balcony is covered in horrific junk

i couldn't quite reach

synonyms: gush, rush, outpouring, stream, flow,
     more?
i miss your mother

typically brief
predicted

you couldn't quite reach

synonyms: increase, rise, growth, upswing,
upsurge, groundswell, escalation, leap, more?
a major deployment of comfort/leaves/branches
thinking a palmful

a powerful rush of emotion or feeling
is okay
being stuck picking wrongly
this spot   this sun

sing along with it, as a surge
the gazebo its perimeter
i carry a cup of thhis:

synonyms: rush, uprush, storm, torrent, blaze,
    outburst, eruption, more?

❋

'a sudden surge of _____'   this is my price

traced only by what's invisible

(a sudden marked increase in voltage or current in an
electric circuit)
hello

: one that stings; specifically : a sharp blow or remark
= a bargain

= a bruised foot
= some empty bottles

: a sharp organ with a poison gland
or otherwise adapted to wound by piercing
and injecting a poison

'adapted to wound'
i follow the branch from blue to orange, duskly

the spring grass = a welt

≠

WHAT WAS / ENFANCE
after Rimbaud

this sun, murder grotto, dune among naked bodies, sky's zero in my glass; think through it. a babbling sound through my days. it flows around me, through the sun, then closer to me.

midnight nails its hour to the wall, at the edge of the room – the dream plant in a pot of gold – beside cups of ink, the plant's contraptions, the silence of the plant and its reaching and aging.

the born moon, the figuring, the forgotten shirt,

and soon i shall have this sound in me. and that sound.

※

here is the closed room, behind the chrysanthemums, the dead little room and its mat of astroturf, the whole sky is luminous (in the room), and the great obstacle is what has already taken place.

genius is this power of dying. her tragic love of life.

you follow hello to the sound of a friend. the castle is now open. you may go inside. *the women who have given themselves are hanged in unbelievable cruelty.* surrounded by smells and rotting meat.

well, all is changed; the desert has come to you. besides, there's
nothing to see.

※

the springs rise and dry, the sunny field is raised without
apologies, the weathercock, crosswinds, and wingspans form
an isthmus to the sun, the sun, the field's headress. the gold
steeple of the desert stretches its arms to the curbs of your
street and needles flowers through your window.

(the talking stones were pissed and murmuring. the astroturf
was growing. zeros were asking no questions as stages on the
way to unrewarded perfection.)

※

in the room, there is a creak, its sound stops you and makes
you quiet.

there is a repetition.
there is the sound of a fountain that is just a sound.
there is a fitted sheet and a gold frame.
there is a patterned glass and there is water in the glass.
there is a blue inkpot and an amber inkpot.
there is a disappearance (the sun).
there is a repetition.

＊

i am the player on the pond, figuring a move, as this year lasts longer than the last.

i am the right structure for the beam of this sun. its drunken laundry setting.

i am the space the cracking sound took. i am opening the moment.

someday, i'll be the length of the shadow of the tree's sad hand.

it's harder to cross here, but when you do, you walk to a narrowing point. it's beautiful if you look at it across the music.

＊

i pay with time because it's precious to me. and the pattern round the glass is red and permanent.

i turn the plant every hour so it grows right. i know the spaces sound between the words.

i close off the room because it is better to say nothing and pay attention to everything else. *three cats and two dogs. their inner melodies.*

✳

at dusk, the angles stack up against the wall; each is a line-up
of art. what it would look like to orchestrate a late dying.
already half skeletal. and the work you got done.

WHAT YOU HAVE

in the four eyes
that look at me
two accept water

to the pavement
i let go what i put up

what happens
when i just agree   at times
in public spaces

now you see me
in my particular life

i know the particular reasons
that left me

❋

i took

the apologists
the sunny field
its isthmus and headdress

(the weathercock
crosswinds

and wingspans)
without apologies

i took

the way the neon snake flickers
awake at night above
the dive across the street

the way the words coil at night

moment of doubt
hello

hello biological
and unfamous
foam on your lip just there
get it

whatever you say
it is an unpleasant emotion
and likely

and have you made your confederation yet
and was it the sand that scalded

✺

what rules the world
is a current medium
of exchange
the intervening substance
it lives and is cultured

i also took
this

✺

the point at
or around
the centre of a period of time
being at
an equal distance
from the extremities
of two other things

(one's family and relations)

✺

it's not a problem

i am sometimes the dolphin
on that necklace
you gave me

the thin silver chain
and its hanging

and the main thing is we begin
she said   with clothing
before we clean beneath the sink

☀

maybe i thought it out

maybe then this is
just a version

the number six woke me up

from a feeling
at the likelihood
of something
unwelcome happening

what you tell love
is strange and tuesday
i was nearly lost

hey

it's a form of athletics
a person's standard of play

or wild mammals or birds
hunted for food

☀

who will i write to as an alien
and snow out on the street

if i am not ready in time
but meant it

i walk the busy street
to the busy line
and the sign i pass

and the *tiger*
tiger scrawled in the sill
of the tram

tiger tiger
we both knew the song
so the day stuck

the sign is primary yellow
its letters are outlines

modern like the mural
we made
of sundaes
and cigarettes

beside the recipe all along

on the sixth i saw several great haircuts
i bought a silver shirt a pink shirt and a polka dot
i took a bath and did not wash my hair
i listened to italian and saw someone read in italian
i heard german and spanish
i humoured
i made pleasant
i felt the pain of the past week and i doubted
i bought a book signed to harold
i evaded a question
i sprung
i saw a silver watch face
i showed off a cover
i said i had a nice time
i answered a question
i thought about aliens
i read about sketches of demons or aliens

i thought about the western imagination (which is severe)
i thought about how the western imagination considers aliens
    (as demons)
i unpacked stone from a plastic bag
i filled my mouth with coloured sugar
i thought about a child
i was terse
i was overwhelmed by words and poor eyesight
i thought about asking when distracted by the body
i thought about the body and its distractions
i dropped the spoon and lid but not the content
i thought it's a long one and will be long   being here now
and alone here

☀

to pay a man for my safety
today i had to

turn around

a stencil of your daydream
i bought it for dreaming

there is so much to say
of your goddess venue
my misunderstanding is
the organization
of the wound's ingredients

you can watch the full thaw

can't offer any more
to the misery of being a body
in the misery of being anything but a body

and the balance
and forcing
i am
to remember what day it was

the flowers died
in the morning i

☀

woke to discomfort

having wanted my case separate
my encasing untouched

and the retaliation of all that

and what did you think you would find there
and what do you want

the powerful imaginary won't leave me
and new birds are coming
and i've reached the corrugation

＊

you've been impressed by the gimmicks
and i hold them to my heart

you've been let down
and i hold it in my palm

you've been gone
and i hold it to my eye

you've been in the long line
and made aware

i will take you back to my ship

the two owls with their backs turned
are made of tiny seashells
the cat's shiny shoulders
are the pink which is the light against pink

＊

i eat sullenly
i drink just a bit of coffee

the flowers sicken
and there is shame here

and disappointment
that simplicity is only a myth
of one's bearing
toward repetition
and stone

come
i will take you back to my ship

[flute]:   heat is a measurable quality and can
                      be treated mathematically
[silence]:   surrounded by unfamiliar art
[heat]:   it passes between a system and its
                      surroundings in some other way than
                      through work
[sun]:   waits on three notes of a flute
[water]:   suitable pathways
[spring]:   a bullet's
[sea]:   calorimetry   a measurable
[stranger]:   relentlessness
[stranger]:   (treated mathematically)
[raymond]:   between grates where people shout to
                      one another
                      more like an artists' colony
[meursault]:   treated as a material substance

two, the sky

THE PURPLING NIGHT IS THE TREES
HEAVY WITH DARKING

is my shelving of its book there on my shelf
as the dog calls in the field, thick with the sky's bidding
perch me back on my table, with my newing
my precious newing, *aloof moon, leave me be*
how i got so comfortable with
a sleepy passing car to marry my fearing
riding round the gazebo   *my nighting*
is the waves of sound in the distance, my fonding
of fear, o communicator, *it hangs like a wet heat*, my limping
dog on my table, so comfortable with it, my blooding
filling my body with heat, wristing
night's folds in the pages, *the trees electricking*
with sundown, a stone building fortifies against the shimmering
which is the unworried night sky pestling me to sugar, my
     anointing
complete, the benches are waiting for it, not differenting
my sorrowed lungs, empty of performance, and the clouding
     pinking
bluing lighting leaving

WHAT IS / AMYNO

hey you, move your car
i am moving

it drew myself a picture
it flew home
it saw me one night and it thought it looked
nice
being terrible
to it
a slight of mind

several
it drew
until it was certain
of my punishability

in the fairy forest
on the wet walk

hello
it is moving
boxed beside the truck

what does it think is wrong with me
i am 'smilingly alive'
smoking
myself out

walking to its house
writing letters
in its bed

take this knife
this spoon, my eagle

at its house i sit on the high wire and clang
walls lined with papers of burnt oil
i run a walkway from my heart to the ground
walk up it
this sound is attached to my body
and thousands of dollars

i like my leather face
my broken tooth
my ripe banana skin
i sit in the sun
i excavate, erase

i hunt me for it
a woodbug in the walls
the exoskeleton rolls beneath the baseboard
and my fat fingers
can't reach it

i ram into the truck
my insides bloom on all the corners
death is cooking
having grown raw
rust transfigures my gaze
and i am annoyed and tin

my heart stamps down the walkway
i am moving

de-skyed erased ungone unshelled
deluged interred unjewelled unsponged
unwed no heat debreathed unshone
distook unslept rewoke rethrown
unwound in void uncold unsunned
resunned in cold devoid rewound
disthrown unwoke reslept retook
reshone rebreathed rethawed rewed
responged rejewelled exhumed embarked
reshelled regone retained in sky

walk 1:

two sentinels, the guard at the end of the lane, the softly ticking
nails of what follows, what surpasses me

take comfort; the pain, it is evenly spaced, and the guard, it guards

the wall here is blue, and my path is blocked by a blue pain; i
reserve it

is it ever good to be as now, under the crags?

i cannot go that way, so i go another

in the glass space of waiting, i get up when i know i must leave

halfway

the way i dance across the way; the way i'm taut at the wheel

my blithe yellow eye, my missing anger – these are the daffodils;
i won't sit long

the pieced-out acid thoughtmeal, you, no place to sit, it rains

surprise, at the place i find myself at, tossing the same trash in
the same can

a wire basket

elvis.ca

a dinosaur in various positions of deadness

a vine slung on electric wire

a old man in sneakers biking into traffic

a lateness

a stain

a pink diagonal walk toward the tree's alveolus

a bony socket

a tooth root

the shot body

the bronchus the vein

the sideways lung trees

the yellow shoot

the brain's banjo cave

(how are you)

the human statue beside the shredded meat

the beds of gold

the took-up lesson

the windpipe the bronchus

the perceptible movement in a direction

the expelled continuous

tooth root

i am moving

THE SUN'S CITIZENS ARE SOLAR NOTES

it comes to set up a mood
the sun, weakly

sun-lung, my tea is cold
the heat is what-without

being is coming up again
and i am spun, under the spun sun

correction: i am my own convection   overwrought
in yellow   i dress in the light
at the bottom of the pool i
ferry light along
here
i am in it

if this moment (nothing) is something to me
i've meant it

the sky sets shut, pulling up its ladder

i am slung in my beam suit
weather-lapelled

pull it up here

i only think in this, like that

i unaccept this too
hand me a beer –
i meant beginning
this shows on the sun

the water is boiling
and ready for steeping
the tub of sugar more bulbous
in the door's knock

these are here and now you
are too irrupting
under touch

ousted by lack of interest   *i am not*
myself(ing)

nightly when i irritate
the mill of my dreams' threads

what does it mean to live a night
like this

be serious

hand me a beer
i end here

it was all worth it since it was
so vastly interesting

sit in sun's snow which is sky
or something serious   love
for the imagined now

over and lived up to, unspared

grow out of this

the bluebell i knew was this,
its alley is mine

the broken glib button was this,
send it to the sun

the seven tongue ties
of your bad day,
throw them to the winds

the broken salt dish, its serious fate,
hurl it for luck

can't turn off a single light
l'installation était ainsi faite:
it was all or nothing

c'est fate

a good day sun, a cactus sun
sends sharp translucent rays
under the skin, pain's singing
sky draws sadness
close to me and plummets
its shining cyclops

multiform me
evolute me
amount

look at the moment   it's joy here
exit nightfall

enter, rough birds
a calm lemon in the sky
the weather's a spirit – *all hazard*
the gentle purple breeze meets
the burial house of noon
warble me   street me

i thought of it

the sun
and

its brought-forth miracle expanding herbage
where can i hang this?

where can i find a house
to perfume it with sundown

[marie]:   old woman staring at her jailed son
[femme]:   nearly perfect sphere   dynamo process
[vieille]:   everyone is moved   my posturing is to myself
[meursault]:   Ra Surya Amaterasu Sól Tōnatiuh
[homme]:   contextualize it   a broken door
[jeune homme]: dung beetle   dung ball sun
[étrangers]:   a way to find words in it

three, women

Country music meets country sky meets grey country road and some mountains. The mountains bring the colour in. Country drums thicken colour to black. New country music starts. The country shows the road is long. The country shows the road is long and already covered with tracks. The diner is full. Its rain is cutlery. Louise, in white. Her ears sling pearls. Guests slip into their seats. Guests sound clatter. Louise serves at the diner. She pours coffee for smirking girls and tells them smoking will kill their sex drive. Louise lights up in the back and someone pours a glass of pure white milk. In the back, Louise tucks a phone to her shoulder. SWITCH. Phone rings at Thelma's. Thelma yells to the quiet – I'll get it. To the quiet, Thelma yells – I've got it. – How are you doing, little housewife. Louise wants to know if sh∼'   ∼ʰed. Thelma says she needs to ask Darryl. Thelma,   ∼l flowers, where noises make the sink water. I   hrist's sake. – Tell him you're going with me. ⅃   ɪelma not to be a child. – Tell him I'm having a ne.   ∼ɑdown. Louise purses her lips at the bright square tank. Louise coaxes the fish from a blush-weave of coral ladders. The camera wobbles as Thelma calls for Darryl after the phone call. A woman on teevee talks about what her nose does to her appearance. – Haven't I told you I can't stand it. Thelma fastens Darryl's watch around his wrist. – When you holler in the morning. Thelma says sorry. Darryl's hand floats beside her neck as she adjusts the watch. Darryl downs something from the fridge. Thelma says Hon. Darryl uses both hands to fix his hair. To fix his hair, Darryl uses both hands. The camera shoots from the illusion of a long mirror, with Darryl his hands soar through the air around his head, but he can't sculpt his hair right. No, he doesn't want a coffee. Thelma says Hon. Darryl halts his hands and takes a

he's pack
robed in paste
Louise says for C
Louise wants Th
rvous brea

deep breath to tamp his rage. Darryl halts his hands to slow-say What. – Do you want anything. Darryl doesn't give a shit. – Special for dinner tonight. He may not make it home tonight. Thelma's onto him as she puts the dish in the sink, under the laminated cleaning instructions. – Funny how many people want to buy a carpet on a Friday night. Thelma shakes the water off a plate. Images of dream kitchens are taped along the kitchen wall. The kitchen's rain is porcelain, settling in the sink. He is beside the bowling trophy and the hung yellow fly swatter. He swings his keys like a yo-yo. Darryl says it's a good thing she's not regional manager … A beat follows the catch … And he is. Outside, the sprinklers confetti off the square patch of lawn around the tiny windmill. The man with the wheelbarrow is between the windmill and t⌐ ⌐ sports car. Darryl hustles in his turquoise blazer. For ⌐ ramps on some plywood beside the red car. A w ck to Darryl points the hose away. Never turns says Jesus and tumbles backward over the plyw⌐ ⌐ the red car. Goddamnit. Christ. He's got to get to work. He doesn't need this bullshit in the morning. For Chrissakes. All the lights on the red car blink when it ignites. Darryl points with his right to the man with the wheelbarrow. He wants them out by five. No, three. The lights blink and the car sounds a low squeal. There's no roof on the car because the sun is out and beaming on Darryl's coiffed head. Darryl pulls out. Darryl is off. In the diner a man picks up the ringing phone. – Thelma, when are you going to run away with me. Louise grabs the phone and says Thelma is running away with her. Thelma holds the phone between her head and her shoulder. She takes a bite out of a bar and puts it back in the fridge. Louise says she's going to bring everything. Thelma opens the fridge to take another bite. Neither of them

the red sp
Chrissakes. St
orker with his ba
around. Darryl
od beside

know how to fish but Darryl does so it can't be hard. Thelma takes a third bite. Louise's Thunderbird is long and turquoise. Her hair is wrapped in a turquoise scarf as she walks across the sheening lot. A woman sings 'Wild Nights.' Thelma's in curlers in her turquoise room. SWITCH. Louise compartmentalizes her mind. Whips open a clear bag for her bone-white Keds. SWITCH. Thelma's dresser holds a magic slipper and a frosted cottage. Thelma rifles through pink and floral. Her nightgown hangs in the window's milk light. Her nightgown's ghost is in the mirror. SWITCH. Louise presses each item gently into her suitcase. Thelma dumps a drawer into her suitcase. SWITCH. Louise chews gum and adjusts her western collar. A left-hand ring holder reaches up beside her mirror. Photo-booth strip taped to the mirror shows a ┐   ⌐ir in black and white in black and white. 'Hey, this is ┐   ` here right now.' Louise tips Jimmy's photo on `   ⌐. Thelma stuffs things into her bags. Its rain ı   ρen drawer sees a little gun. Beside the gun, a boo.   ⌐ Time, holds wild country mystery and a lost woman. SWITCH. Louise, in the kitchen window milk-light. A sponge stack beside the sink. A lone blue cup to rinse. SWITCH. Thelma picks up the gun like it's a worm and drops it in her bag. SWITCH. Louise buffs the cup. Colour is stacked in the window light. Louise's cutting board is nearly imperceptible. She moves to reveal a shiny faucet, the ordered sponges, a pale folded cloth, and a blue cup. SWITCH. The turquoise Thunderbird pulls up and honks for Thelma. The sprinklers soften. Louise smiles gorgeously. She gets out to put Thelma's lantern back since they will have electricity. Louise, in white. Thelma's jean jacket slings pearls. She holds a turquoise net. Thelma keeps the lantern in case of a loose killer killing electricity. Louise says in that case the lantern could

lost pai
Jimmy. I'm not
his face. SWITCI
s clutter. The o
k, *A Thief of*

come in real handy. Louise's hair is tucked in a scarf. Thelma's hair is a mane. They have almost got everything in the car so Louise smiles gorgeously. Thelma puts the net in last. The sprinklers on the lawn are off. They take a Polaroid as the Thunderbird's trunk closes. The photo freezes the smiles for a moment. As they drive, Thelma throws up her hands and whoops. There are new sprinklers in the corner of the shot. Louise tells Thelma to sit down. Thelma puts on her shades. – Oh, Louise, can you take care of this gun? Louise wants to know what the hell she brought it for. Killers, bears, snakes. Thelma puts the gun in Louise's purse. – Thelma, good lord. They talk about where they are going. Thelma has never been out of town without Darryl. She takes off her jacket. Her shoulders are ghost-bare and ' '-ess is long and white. Louise asks why Darryl let The˙   ɔ didn't ask him. – Shit, Thelma. Louise laughs   kill you. Darryl never lets Thelma do one goc   ɔ's any fun. She left him a note. – Left him stuff to ı.   . Thelma and Louise laugh. A herd of cows gallop dust over the screen. A woman sings. SWITCH. Louise takes a drag. Thelma sets her bare feet on the dash. Louise reproaches her. Thelma puts her feet down. Louise frowns and takes a drag. Thelma adjusts the side view so she is in it. Takes a fake drag and adjusts her shades. 'Hey, I'm Louise.' They hit a crossroads. Thelma wants to stop for a minute. She takes a bite out of a bar. Louise says they'll never get to the cabin till after dark as it is. Thelma itches her nose. Says, come on, I never get to do stuff like this. Louise says it's going to be a quick stop. A big truck wets the roads. Louise swerves to avoid being sprayed. Thelma or Louise lets out a little scream. Mist and glare shroud the night street. Thelma and Louise enter the fluorescent lot. Glow and din inside the

d her dre
lma go. Thelm
s. – He's going to
damn thing tha
microwave.

Silver Bullet. Fuchsia gloom hovers over the billiards. The bar's rain is laughter and knock, a haze of faces, but Louise moves through the light. She hasn't seen a place like this since Texas. Thelma thinks it's fun. Louise is quiet. A woman sings. They move through the light and end up at a table. The server has a pink belt and a plunge of fringe. She asks if y'all want a drink. Louise says no, thanks. Thelma wants a Wild Turkey straight up and a Coke back. Thelma says Louise's as bad as Darryl. Thelma says look out 'cause her hair is coming down. Louise changes her mind, orders a margarita and a shot of Cuervo on the side. Thelma takes her shot – Hey! What are a couple of Kewpie dolls like you doing in a place like this? a man asks. Thelma says they left town for the weekend. Louise says minding our own business, whv [illegible] you try? Thelma says 'cause they wanted to try to h [illegible] The server returns with drinks. Says Harlan, ar [illegible] hese poor girls? Harlan says hell no. He was ju [illegible]. Server says it's a good thing they're not all as frie [illegible] n. Louise nods and takes a drag. Thelma has an uncle named Harlan. Harlan says if he's a funny uncle, they have something in common. Harlan touches Thelma's knee when he laughs. Louise blows her smoke in Harlan's face. Says she doesn't mean to be rude but she has something she needs to talk to her friend about in private. Harlan looks Louise straight in the eye. He slow-says he understands. Says he didn't mean to bother them, and looks at Thelma. – But it's hard not to notice such pretty ladies as themselves. Thelma sucks her drink through a straw and smiles. Harlan says she'd better dance with him before she leaves or he will never forgive her. He winks. Half of his face enters shadow when he stands. A single eyebrow looms. Thelma says sure that'd be fun. Harlan leaves. Louise holds her cigarette straight

don't y
ave some fun.
e you bothering t
st being friendly
ndly as him

and takes a swig of her margarita. Says, can't you tell when somebody is hitting on you? Thelma thinks it's all Louise's years of waiting on tables that's made her jaded, that's all. The band starts playing. Thelma takes a shot. Thelma jumps and claps, yells woo! A man sings in thick blue haze. A painting of a horse is behind him. Thelma waves at Harlan. Thelma wonders if Darryl's home yet. Louise wonders if Jimmy ever got back. Thelma thinks Louise should tell him to get lost once and for all. Louise thinks Thelma should ditch that no-good-husband-of-hers. Harlan orders Thelma and Louise another round. Harlan smiles at Thelma across the room. Thelma knows when Jimmy comes in off the road and Louise won't be there, he'll freak out and call her a hundred thousand times. Sunday night she'll call him back, and by ᴺ ⸍ ¹ᵛ Jimmy will be kissing the ground she walks on. E⸲   ise. They decide to have some fun and take an   ˙ make whiskey hoots. Harlan waves. Thelma ₅   ₍helma disappears with Harlan. A blue shroud o₁   ₋₀ves alongside the band. The singer's hair hangs past his shoulders. SWITCH. Harlan asks for Thelma's name. The fluorescent beam cuts through Harlan's head. – Follow me, Thelma. Thelma says she doesn't know what she's doing. Harlan's arm is around Thelma's neck. He holds a beer by the throat as he spins her. The light cuts through his head. Thelma laughs. Behind her is pastel dream light. SWITCH. Louise smokes at table, beside two full margaritas. A man approaches to ask if she wants to dance a little. Sure, says Louise. Louise's dance partner wears a flowered black shirt. She looks for Thelma as she dances. Louise pretends to relax. Louise dances. SWITCH. Harlan holds Thelma very close. He holds his beer tight to Thelma's neck. Harlan dips Thelma. Harlan tells Thelma she's got some great moves. A voice yells

Monday
xactly, says Lou
other shot. They
ays let's dance.
f dancers m

ALL RIGHT, HERE WE GO, HERE WE GO, HERE WE GO.
Harlan dips Thelma. SWITCH. The boots stomp out a dance.
Thelma smiles in the line dance beside Harlan. She spins before
everyone else. Her left hand holds a beer. Harlan's expression
is serious. The camera wobbles between lines of distant faces.
The camera is short and drunk. A woman at the end of the line
claps and sways her hips dashboard-style. Heavy boots kick
the air. SWITCH. The line turns. Harlan is behind Thelma.
When the dance finishes, he pulls her hips toward his. The
camera finds Louise who says thanks and leaves the dance floor.
Her partner trails after, hands on his hips. He disappears. Louise
is stern as she moves back to the table. She takes a sip of her
untouched margarita. Her shoulders sigh. Harlan spins Thelma.
Harlan spins Thelma. *Harl~ ·¹·~ true recipient.* Harlan spins
Thelma. Thelma is dru·   dizzy. Thelma falls into
Harlan and salutes Lo·   :ety beer. *Thelma takes*
the shape of Harlan's co   ~als Thelma by tapping
her watch with her ciga~   *.egation is felt as suffering.*
Thelma falls into Harlan. Louise gets up with her purse. Arrives.
Harlan spins Thelma. Hey, hey, Thelma, says Louise. Thelma
laughs. I'm hitting the girls' room then we're out of here, says
Louise. Harlan dips Thelma. I'm ready when you are, laughs
Thelma. Thelma's head sways as if unattached. Thelma says wait
Louise. I want to come with you. Harlan grunts and spins
Thelma. Turn around, Harlan says. I don't feel so good, says
Thelma. What's wrong, says Harlan. Come on, says Harlan.
Thelma drops her beer. Shit, she says. Stop, she says. She stares
at the ground. She totters. She leans over and takes a breath.
Her hair is sweat-wet. I'm spinning, she says. Harlan yanks her
chin. Oopsy-doopsy, he says. We need to get you some fresh
air, little lady. Harlan glances at the exit. He breathes heavily,

an is the

nk. Thelma is

uise with her rick

tact. Louise sig

ette. *Her n*

dripping sweat. Harlan puts his hand on Thelma's neck. SWITCH. Harlan guides Thelma out of the bar with his hands on her hips. She stumbles. Louise is in the smoke-hazed ladies' room packed with women. All the women have turquoise shadow under their eyes. Louise is sober in a drunk sea. She shakes the water off her hands, smoothes the skin on her face, and stares at her reflection. She turns to make her way out. Bitch, someone says. Louise glides through the bar and stops back at her table. Look, have you seen my friend, asks Louise. Your friend? the server says. Yeah, yeah, she was out there dancing, the server says. Louise waves her off. SWITCH. The camera stalks the dark lot. Its eye is low among the vehicles. In the dark Harlan's voice says, how are you feeling now, darling. Thanks, Thelma says. I thir^ ^ ^tarting to feel a little better. *An impression is an effect ^* ^amera pauses at Thelma and Harlan between t ^ leans on one with his arm in front of Thelma. ^ is on his hip. She wipes her face with a handkerch. ^ ^tarting to feel pretty good to me too, he says. You know that? He leans his head toward her. She leans away from him. She pushes him softly. I think I need to keep walking, she says. She wipes her brow. Wait a minute. Wait a minute. Wait a minute, he says. He grabs her arm and steps in front of her. Where do you think you're going, huh. The camera is over his shoulder looking at her face. Her eyes are closed. I'm going back inside, she says. Oh no, no, he says. *An impression is a belief.* He lifts her onto the trunk of the car. She lets out a little scream. Harlan, she says. What, he says and starts lifting up her skirt. Hey, quit it, stop it, stop it, she says. He doesn't stop. Thelma, Thelma, listen to me. Listen to me, he says. She sniffs. I'm not going to hurt you, okay, he says. I just want to kiss you, he says. All right, he says. No, no, she

k I'm s
on *feelings*. The
wo cars. Harlan
His other hand
ief. You're s

says. Come on, come on, come on, he says. He leans in very slowly to kiss her frozen cheek. Goddamn, you are gorgeous, he says, looking at her lap. All right, let me go now, come on, she says. She pushes his shoulder. She tries to stop his hands from pushing her skirt up. The camera sees her thighs. He stands between her knees. Let me go, I mean, I'm married, she says. Come on, she says. She struggles. He laughs, that's okay, I'm married too. *An impression is an imitation or an image.* He pulls at her sleeves around her shoulders. I don't feel good, I've been sick, she says. She pushes him harder. He slaps her across the face and holds his finger up. Listen to me, he says. I'm not going to hurt you, all right, he says. Relax, he says and starts unbuttoning her top. *Hardness is his orientation.* Harlan, stop it, she says. Please, I mean it, sh⸍   ⸍He starts ripping her clothes. Thelma sobs. Wait. Don'   ⸜ says. *His emotion shapes her body as a form of ac*   ing to wonder where I am, she says. Harlan's f⸠   ⸍. Fuck Louise, he says. Fuck. *His emotion shapes*   *⸍face of her body.* She slaps him across the face. His face is revulsion and hatred. HEY, he says and slaps her powerfully across her face. Her head swings and her eyes go out of focus. *An impression is a mark on the surface.* Thelma screams. He slaps the other side of her face. DON'T EVER FUCKING HIT ME, he says. FUCKING BITCH, he says. He slams her face onto the car and holds her hands behind her back. *Hatred circulates the sheening lot.* He pulls her skirt over her ass. He starts to pull off her underwear. He rips his belt off. Don't hurt me, Harlan, please, she says. SHUT UP, he says. He pulls down his underwear. SHUT THE FUCK UP, he says. YOU HEAR ME. Drool falls from his mouth. She is sobbing. SHUT UP, he says. Please, she says. He shakes her head violently against the car. *Fear shapes the surface*

he says.

t. I mean it, she

tion. Louise is go

ace is full and re

the very sur

of her skin. Please, she says. Please don't hurt me, Harlan, she says. GODDAMN BITCH, he says. The camera watches Thelma's sobbing face. There are specks of blood on her jean jacket. Harlan is ripping off her underwear. The camera looks at his face. *His hatred produces her.* Don't hurt me, Harlan, please, she says. The camera looks at her white sandals with his black boots between them. Harlan kicks her feet further apart. Thelma screams. Get the fuck out of here, says Harlan. The camera sees Thelma's bare ass. Harlan is struggling with her underwear. Louise, screams Thelma. Harlan scowls at Thelma. Louise's hand appears. *Her feeling shapes the gun.* Louise shoves hatred under Harlan's left ear. You let her go, you fucking asshole, she says. Or I'm going to splatter your ugly face all over this nice car. The camera looks at Lo··· ᴗuise stares at Harlan's neck. *Contact involves the subj⸍ histories that come before the subject.* Harlan slov helma grabs her jacket and moves behind Lou. ⸍. Louise lowers the gun an inch and Harlan almoѕ⸜ ᴗise shoves the gun deeper into his neck. All right, hey, hey, hey, just calm down, says Harlan. Thelma sobs. We were just having a little fun, that's all, says Harlan. Looks like you got a real fucked-up idea of fun, says Louise. Harlan winces. Come on, come on, Thelma sobs. Louise backs up with her eyes on Harlan and the gun pointed straight at his heart. The camera approaches Louise's face. Turn around, says Louise. Harlan turns around. He is annoyed. Louise looks at his face. *He is soaked in affect … What sticks?* In the future, when a woman's crying like that, she isn't having any fun, says Louise. Thelma sobs. Louise turns to walk away. BITCH, says Harlan. I should've gone ahead and fucked her. Louise turns. *How pain feels in the first place is an effect of past impressions, often hidden from view.* What did you say? asks

se. Lo

ect, involves the

ly backs off as T

se. Thelma sobs

turns. Lou

Louise. *It is this perceived intrusion of something other within the body that creates the desire to re-establish the border, to push out the pain, or the (imagined, material) object we feel is the 'cause' of the pain.*

I said suck
my
cock.

[louise]:   indoors, the flower's yellow head blooms as
ice thrives on the glass and blankness fills the
lace of ice

[thelma]:   *in the street, a stranger wants to see me and i can't
say no*

[louise]:   being a borderless amethyst's lucid dream

[thelma]:   *propelling my addiction, which are human things
maybe*

[louise]:   sleeping in the room with you

[thelma]:   *some invented words for a system*

[louise]:   in which i lose, finding again the sentence as it
runs by me –

[thelma]:   *finding again the night sky pestling us to sugar*

[louise]:   finding again ≠

four, flowers

JACKPOT

i've never been to jackpot nevada but i intend to go. panting. i can't tell if my neighbours can see me through their windows and it bothers me. can't live in a world without men but that's not the point. i was married once yes and very rich. my daughter lives in nevada. in nevada where the cacti get the shadows right. by my home is a big blue steeple. it looks strange like a house, water tower, or mill. an eight-year-old threw dice to predict my future (chaotic evil). just take a look at me. i pretended i was anne sexton once and read her work to a crowd. no i do not hate my mother. but my daughter's far away. a fly walks the circumference of my leg. picks the shin. unconsciousness is the sun burning my chest in which the dog cannot be stimulated to be awakened. near the roof. i know i'll need to remove the legs to move the table. people get very busy with their excessive environmental heat and this includes me.

i've never been to jackpot nevada but i intend to go. panting. i can't tell if my nerves can see me through my wine and it bothers me. can't live in a wound without manuals but that's not the point. i was married once yes and very rich. my dawn lives in nevada. in nevada where the cacti get the shapes right. by my honeysuckle is a big blue steeple. it looks strange like a house-wife, wave, or miracle. an eight-year-old threw dice to predict my gain (chaotic evolution). just take a look at me. i pretended i was anne sexton once and read her point to a crystal. no i do not hate my motif. but my dawn is far away. a focus wanders the circumference of my legacy. picks the shin. unconsciousness is the supermarket burning my childhood in which the domain cannot be stimulated to be awakened. near the roof. i know i'll need to remove the legacy to move the taste. people get very busy with their excessive environmental hedges and this includes me.

i've never been to jackpot nevada but i intend to go. panting. i can't tell if the newcomers can see me through their wisdom and it bothers me. can't live in a yard without a map but that's not the point. i was married once yes and very rich. my dear lives in nevada. in nevada where the cacti get the shelter right. by my horse is a big blue steeple. it looks strange like a hunting weekend, traffic, or a minister. an eight-year-old threw dice to predict my garment (chaotic excuse). just take a look at me. i pretended i was anne sexton once and read her polymer to a curve. no i do not hate my mount. but my dear is far away. a folly wardrobes the circumference of my leisure. picks the shin. unconsciousness is the supper burning my chocolate in which the donor cannot be stimulated to be awakened. near the roof. i know i'll need to remove the liabilities to move the taxation. people get very busy with their excessive environmental herbs and this includes me.

i've never been to jackpot nevada but i intend to go. panting. i can't tell if my nights can see me through their withdrawals and it bothers me. can't live in a year without march but that's not the point. i was married once yes and very rich. my death lives in nevada. in nevada where the cacti get the shame right. by my hour is a big blue steeple. it looks strange like humour, a weapon, or a mirror. an eight-year-old threw dice to predict my gaze (chaotic exhibition). just take a look at me. i pretended i was anne sexton once and read her poetry to a cry. no i do not hate my mountain. but my death is far away. a forest watches the circumference of my liberty. picks the shin. unconsciousness is the sunlight burning my child in which the dolphin cannot be stimulated to be awakened. near the roof. i know i'll need to remove the lessons to move the talent. people get very busy with their excessive environmental hell and this includes me.

a work of art is
a   confession
someone   said
was   worth   25
~~dollars~~ flowers
when   we   see
things clearly we
only   have   one
thing to say *we are
up on the roof with
the sun all in it*
the vanity of the
word *experience*
moving too fast
a   setting   a
neighbourhood
and   its
accidental
connections
(inhabitants) the
mother   and
what she does

(an assessment)
storm sky in
august have we
squealed enough
in the wind of it
in gusts of hot
wind do we
write knowing
anger in black
clouds in the
asphodel field the
alarmist
table
sitting at it

coming together the
body   temperature
must   be   lowered
quickly *where are we
going*   clothing
removed   to
promote heat loss
bear it on the surface
bathed   in   cold
water *anyone can do
it* cold compresses
to the torso head
neck   and   groin
*getting so close you
expect things* a fan
dehumidifying   the
evaporation   of
water *what is this* to
move   instinctually
instead (evaporative
method)   swallow
when it hurts a tub
of cold water *we think
of you – we can*

be alone without your
feeling (immersion
method)
differentiate
between person and
woman (the effort
of several people)
take our own care
head held above
water the ability to
keep immersion in
very cold water let
down (what is this)
reduced blood flow
when the bird's
outside the window
we swear it looks in at
us escaping the
body core to always
have to get the facts
straight um
challenged in
experimental
studies *we don't need*
this cutaneous
vasoconstriction not
the best shivering
thermogenesis can't
just drop everything

do not play a
dominant role *drop
everything* bodily
defences slow to
keep from us the
ultimate fail to
maintain *is this
what you abolished*
shuddering what
we got ourselves
into with the *too
much* no individual
effects *what's going
to do with it* a lack of
response get old a
little to the left
aggressive
immersion hand it
to you the gold
bouquet do we
want this hydration
is of paramount
importance no one
gave up too soon
but absorption is
rapid and complete
condition
reassessed

something tenderer
a flower drained of
colour   *heart   rate*
and breathing mistook
for love

the real climate of
tragedy is heat on
the quays not the
night is it always
about getting it
right?   perfect
madness   is   a
beautiful setting for
a morning (use
language and it
gets colder) *the
doomster rose is
shedding her body*
the sun is gone (go
on inside) the tops
of buildings get a
little colder with all
the   damning
evidence in our
hands we're afraid
of   punishment
we're glad this
went   nowhere

it's perfect here
so everyone
should be happy
moving away
from their bodies
we are trying to
be more
imperative
retrieve pieces
the wind blows
petals through
my window *are*
we resisting? ~~they~~
~~say those who~~
~~hear voices~~ we
say we use our
right hands for
most things and
that's why they're
fucked in the
morning we are
in your lash we

are in your
eyelash at times
our lungs only
partly fill and
when the screen
is open things
enter some days
we ask is my
chair facing the
wrong way or is
it me then
conclude there
are two things in
this world um we
friend intensities
we guess a video
of a woman
sucking a plastic
bag over her face
we sit in the
bedstraw in the
city park we
write a line of
poetry it goes *we
run our hands
through your
spaghetti screaming
that we meant to*

what   interests
people in a work
are signs of a
sorrowful
existence
someone laughs
outside the door
then sends a letter
'to make her feel
sorry' we come
home two and a
half years later
but our bones
break in the
middle of it 'we
are good to you
and you are doing
us wrong' on this
side of words we
ask for space and
we give it the
temperature
varies from this
moment to the
next cause *by
space we meant
galaxy*

we decide to steal
something then
decide not to
everywhere's a
thin film of
sunlight (put it
back on the shelf)
we try to reach
ourselves it's
chilling *it is at the*
heart of this light
that we are to be
found

is it wrong to
waste time we
waste our time all
day long to finish
it a cloud passes in
the shape of a rose
and we die to
ourselves but we
resist silence *we are
tipsy with suffering
cause it's made up of
the sun* what did
we decide to call it
um moment of
adorable silence
unlike you what
we want is happy
unawareness

everyone knows
it's about you
we would call your
pessimism *solar* a
day of sunshine
and clouds we
ought to keep a
diary of each
day's weather a
title *the hope of the*
world

we found a book
of humour (what is
this?) a long walk
kept it for later
smiles jokes and
plans don't let them
stop *we are linked to
the world by
everything we do* we
let a voice put us to
sleep moving the
grass and sunlight
climb the hill

the sun is doing
us a lot of good it
grows us flowers
shines   directly
overhead   the
glare's unbearable
this is who we are
we   award
experiments   one
foot on the sill *you*
weren't   thinking
about   anything   in
those   delicate
moments   because
the sun was beating
down on your bare
head   closing
around   until
consciousness
slipped   we

imagine   being
with you in the
red sand blazing
we never noticed
how the windows
pile   high   above
one another high
above   one
another   and
overlook   the
buildings we wish
you were here to
dance to it the
sun   shatters   on
the   sand   a
pointed   gun
waiting   for   the
run-out   in   the
margins of things
mostly pages we
have a face with
seven   holes   *we*
need visible signs

we are too strong
for what you
imagine us to be
(not what we'd
expect) find us a
better shirt for the
untucked a fortune
cookie that says *you
will not get what you
deserve* let out the
line little by little
make a thing of it
think better of it we
want magic we
suggested antlers
full of flowers
the heart of the dog
running in its
dreams

the mess's in the
nook call it off *let
us watch* we study
movement can't
be   taught   the
astrological
swing   despite
trying from this
life we take the
aloneness   we
enjoy work the
soil in the cold
stand as long as
we want *it was
just a hand that a
hand needed in a
hand*   such   a
happy poppy for
once ask for the
dosage by heart
*the flame's aloof
bullet proof just
shoot it*

the struggle with
one's body (keep it
for later) the sun
sucks up the water
and the people
across the water
they see us in all
our silence
we will protest to
the table *we meant
end* the sun among
the five minutes to
make noises *we
meant flowers*
concrete
description
disappearance of
ideas *we meant
friends* what you
do in life is
interesting we
count

one
the sun
two
the sky

Because the Sun takes inspiration from a decade-long fascination with a scene in Albert Camus's *L'étranger* – the one in which his main character Meursault, 'press[ed]' by the blinding sun, shoots a man on the beach. I wanted to take up the relentless heat of the sun and its potential for transference – in this case, from atmosphere to human interaction, from Meursault's murder of the unnamed 'Arab' to the example of gendered violence committed against the victim's sister (also unnamed), and finally the micro-aggressions against Meursault's girlfriend Marie. I saw a parallel here between atmosphere and violence in the 1991 film *Thelma & Louise* – what is it that moves Louise to pull the trigger on Thelma's assailant after Thelma is safe? In both cases, the sun is a material symbol of pain, an affective backlog we're slung under, pushing us through desert after desert, where we become deadly.

I gave voice to the speaker of *Because the Sun*, in part, by weaving excerpts from Camus's extensive notebooks (scoured for every instance in which he refers to the sun), with the surreal lyric of automatic writing, scientific descriptions of heat and heat stroke, and film dictations. *Because the Sun*'s pastiche of personal and 'objective' (often scientific) voices strives to embody both stylistic and formal 'relentlessness' by teasing out discursive tonalities that blend and merge into each other, generating a blinding effect, like looking into the sun.

The italicized lines in *three, women* are either direct quotes or adaptations of lines from Sara Ahmed's seminal work *The Cultural Politics of Emotion* (New York: Routledge, 2014).

The final version of 'Jackpot' was inspired by the Oulipo game N+7, in which you replace the nouns in your original poem with the nouns seven entries below in the dictionary.

Translated quotes from Albert Camus's notebooks (*Notebooks 1935–1942*, Trans. Philip Thody, Chicago: Ivan R. Dee, 2010) are woven throughout the book but especially into the final manifesto: *four, flowers*. The epigraph was also taken from this text.

Cyril Connolly cites an interview in which Jean-Paul Sartre describes Camus's pessimism as '"solar" if you remember how much black there is in the sun' in his introduction to Stuart Gilbert's translation of *The Stranger* (London: Hamish Hamilton, 1946).

The Counterpoint poems are inspired by Deborah Weagel's study of *L'étranger*[7] that locates instances of musical counterpoint in the novel (melodies playing in conjunction with one another), in which the heat and the sun act as instruments.

Thelma & Louise is an outlaw film written by Callie Khouri that lead actors Geena Davis and Susan Sarandon thought would 'revolutionize the film industry'[8] for women, but didn't.

7. Deborah Weagel, 'Musical Counterpoint in Albert Camus's "L'étranger,"' *Journal of Modern Literature* 25, no. 2 (2001–2002): 141–145.

8. Nigel M. Smith, 'Susan Sarandon and Geena Davis: Hollywood hasn't had an epiphany since *Thelma & Louise*,' *Guardian*, May 16, 2016, https://www.theguardian.com/film/2016/may/16/susan-sarandon-geenadavis-hollywood-thelma-louise-feminist-gender-equality.

ACKNOWLEDGEMENTS

Deep gratitude and thanks to the following friends and mentors who supported me through this project and provided invaluable guidance: Hilary Bergen, Paige Cooper, Julia de Montigny, Alonso Gamarra, Jessie Jones, Julie Joosten, Kasia Juno, Jessi MacEachern, Madeleine Maillet, Jeff Noh, Gail Scott, Karen Solie, and Will Vallières.

Thank you to Lisa Robertson who edited this manuscript with erudition and care both at its initial and finishing stages. What an incredible honour.

Thanks very much to Alana Wilcox, Crystal Sikma, and James Lindsay at Coach House, who were such a pleasure to work with.

Thank you to Joani Tremblay for the generous use of her artwork for the cover of this book, and for the walks and conversations about Camus. You can find some paintings inspired by this book at joanitremblay.com, under the exhibit entitled 'The whole time, the sun.' The show took place at Harper's Gallery in Chelsea, New York, and the exhibition text 'How Do You Own the Sun?' is also in conversation with this book.

And thank you to Jordan Robson-Cramer for encouraging me to channel some of my creative energy and outlaw-enthusiasm into country music singing ...

This project began during a writing residency at the Banff Centre and was generously funded by the Canada Council for the Arts. Sections of it have appeared on or in *MuseMedusa*,

Periodicities, and *Drunken Boat Blog*. Many thanks to the faculty, fellow writers, jurors, and editors.

ABOUT THE AUTHOR

Sarah Burgoyne is an experimental poet. Her first collection, *Saint Twin* (Mansfield, 2016), was a finalist for the A. M. Klein Prize in Poetry (2016), awarded a prize from L'Académie de la vie littéraire (2017), and shortlisted for a Canadian ReLit Award. Other works have appeared in journals across Canada and the U.S., have been featured in scores by American composer J. P. Merz, and have appeared within or alongside the visual art of Susanna Barlow, Jamie Macaulay, and Joani Tremblay. She currently lives and writes in Montreal.

Typeset in Arno and Futura.

Printed at the Coach House on bpNichol Lane in Toronto, Ontario, on Zephyr Antique Laid paper, which was manufactured, acid-free, in Saint-Jérôme, Quebec, from second-growth forests. This book was printed with vegetable-based ink on a 1973 Heidelberg KORD offset litho press. Its pages were folded on a Baumfolder, gathered by hand, bound on a Sulby Auto-Minabinda, and trimmed on a Polar single-knife cutter.

Coach House is on the traditional territory of many nations including the Mississaugas of the Credit, the Anishnabeg, the Chippewa, the Haudenosaunee, and the Wendat peoples and is now home to many diverse First Nations, Inuit, and Métis peoples. We acknowledge that Toronto is covered by Treaty 13 with the Mississaugas of the Credit. We are grateful to live and work on this land.

Edited by Lisa Robertson
Cover and interior design by Crystal Sikma
Cover art, *Lemons for Catherine* by Joani Tremblay
Sun photo by Sarah Burgoyne
Author photo by Laurence Philomène

Coach House Books
80 bpNichol Lane
Toronto, ON M5S 3J4
Canada

416 979 2217
800 367 6360

mail@chbooks.com
www.chbooks.com